# Pub walks
# Padstow to Hartland

## Paul White

## Bossiney Books

First published 2011 by Bossiney Books Ltd,
33 Queens Drive, Ilkley, LS29 9QW
www.bossineybooks.com

ISBN 978-1-906474-27-0

**Acknowledgements**
The maps are by Graham Hallowell. Cover based on a design by Heards
Design Partnership. All photographs are by the author.

Printed in Great Britain by R Booth Ltd, Penryn, Cornwall

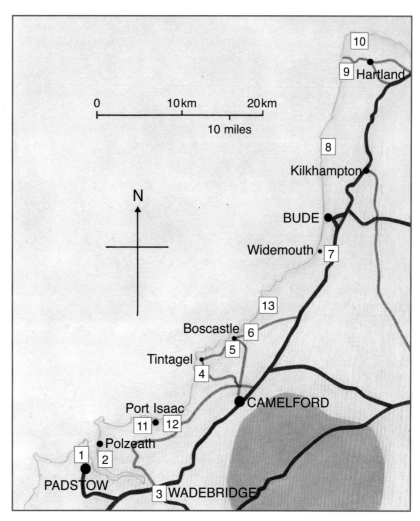

*The approximate locations of the walks in this book*

All the walks in this book were checked prior to publication, at which time the instructions were correct. However, changes can occur in the countryside over which neither the author nor publisher has any control – signposts may disappear, and stiles are sometimes replaced by gates, for example – and alas it is not unknown these days for pubs to cease trading.
Please let us know if you encounter any serious problems.

# Introduction

The walks in this book are all between 8.2 and 12.7 km in length (5 to 7¾ miles) and can be walked in a day. All are circular, and most consist of a stretch of the coast path with an inland return. Some are quite strenuous: the coastal path climbs and descends steeply in places. It might be wise to start with the shorter or easier walks if you are out of practice.

All the walks have at least one pub either on the circuit or at the end. The walks have been selected for their own quality rather than that of the catering, but I hope you won't be disappointed by the pubs either! The parking suggested is always on public land: if you want to use the pub's car park, please check with the landlord before you do so.

## Safety

Proper walking boots are vital on the coast path for grip and ankle support, and I find a walking pole or stick is useful, especially for the steeper descents. On the inland sections in particular you may well find muddy patches even in dry weather, not to mention briars, thistles and nettles, all of which thrive in our soil, so bare legs are a liability.

Cliff walking can be very exposed: the wind-chill factor is like being out in the Atlantic, and of course Cornish weather can change very swiftly, so you need to carry extra layers of clothing as well as waterproofs, for what is often an abrupt change of temperature between inland and cliff walking.

The main hazard of walking the cliff path is that for most of the way it is not fenced off from the drop. Go no nearer the edge than you have to: you might be standing on an overhang. Take great care when the path does take you near the edge, and keep a close eye on children and dogs. In many places the cliffs are eroding, so please respect diversions.

The maps provided look attractive but they are only intended as sketch maps, so you may want to carry an OS 1:25,000 map.

Despite many pressures on their livelihoods, Cornish farmers are still trying to make a living from the land you pass through. Please respect their crops. If the route of a footpath has not been properly restored, please go round the edge of the field. Leave gates closed or open as you find them, and keep dogs under control, especially during the lambing season.

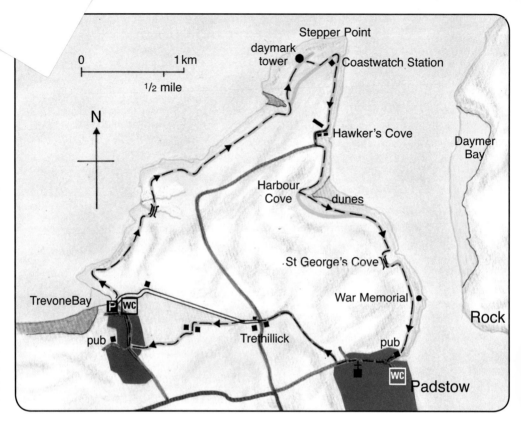

## Walk 1 Trevone and Padstow

*Distance: 12.7 km (7³/₄ miles)*
*Time: 3¹/₄ hours*
*Character: A simple circuit but very attractive, with considerable*
*variety – starting with Atlantic cliffs (some steep ascents), then views*
*over the Camel estuary, usually with exposed sand, the relative bustle*
*of the harbourside at Padstow with many and varied opportunities for*
*refreshment, and an inland return by quiet lanes and footpaths.*

Whilst you could start at Padstow, I prefer to start from Trevone Bay, where there is a beach car park (SW 892760). Head north past the back of the bay, turn left COAST PATH HAWKER'S COVE VIA STEPPER POINT, and simply follow the coast path to Stepper Point.

From the daymark tower, cut across on the main path heading to the right of the Coastwatch Station, then turn left to pass in front of it.

At Hawker's Cove, walk along the access drive around the Cove then turn left down steps, COAST PATH. Follow the path when it heads

*Above: The beach at Trevone Bay*

*Below: The dunes at Harbour Cove*

inland at Harbour Cove, then double back when the opportunity arises, and take the path along the top of the dunes. At the end of the dunes, climb the slope and rejoin the official coast path.

Continue to Padstow Harbour. Padstow has a number of pubs to choose from, and I've not sampled them all! The most obvious – and the first you come to – is The Shipwrights on the harbourside.

From the back of the harbour, head inland up a narrow pedestrianised street, MARKET STRAND, and continue ahead up DUKE STREET. Keep left at a fork by the Cross House Hotel and walk past the parish church. Ignore the first turning on the right, Tregirls Road, and take the next right, a quiet lane, past the entrance to Prideaux Place.

5

*The Shipwrights Arms, and (below) Lanadwell Street, with two of Padstow's oldest pubs, the London Inn and the Golden Lion.*

*A guidebook of 1892 said of Padstow: 'This little town was formerly of some commercial importance, and had a considerable shipbuilding business, but its glory has departed... It is a mean-looking place, of woe-begone aspect... We imagine no-one deliberately visits Padstow for its own sake...' How times have changed!*

When you reach the hamlet of Trethillick, continue ahead on a track then bear right. After 170m, bear left, PUBLIC FOOTPATH. This well-walked path leads across fields, past a cottage (turn left after the cottage, then shortly right over a wooden stile) and onto a lane in Trevone.

If you wish to visit the Well Parc, a hotel and pub, continue ahead on the lane, then ahead at the next junction. Otherwise, turn right down the lane back to the beach car park.

## Walk 2   Rock and Polzeath

*Distance:  11 km (7 miles)*
*Time:  2³/4 hours*
*Character: A flat and easy walk, in an area popular with tourists and second home owners, so you'll see more people than on most of the other walks, but it's peaceful nevertheless. The Camel estuary is beautiful at all stages of the tide.*

Although the walk could be started from Rock or Polzeath, I preferred to start from Daymer Bay, leaving part of the coast path as the finale.

From the Daymer Bay car park (seasonal café and shop, public toilets) take the coast path to the right and follow it round towards Polzeath. When you reach the Tristram car park, turn left to circuit its lower edge. On reaching the road, turn left.

Pass the public toilets, cross the stream and turn right just before a row of flat-roofed shops into an unsigned access drive. Pass a caravan park and continue on a NO THROUGH ROAD. It becomes a track and ultimately crosses a stream and arrives at a golf course.

Turn left and keep the hedge on your left. After 50 m the path ducks through the hedge and continues in the same direction. Ignore side turnings, cross fairways with care and you will reach a housing development. Turn right up the tarmac driveway, and keep right at junctions.

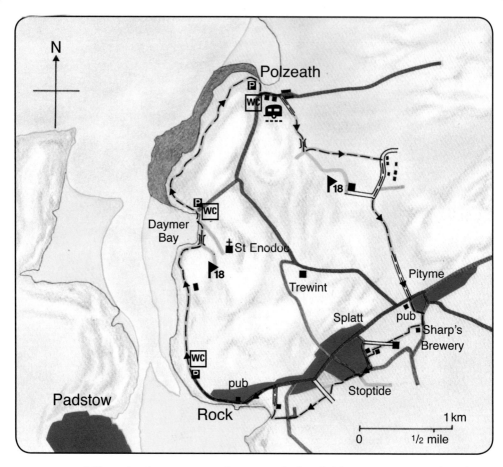

When the drive turns right, towards the clubhouse, continue ahead on a track. Cross another part of the golf course and continue in a southerly direction up a field with the wire fence on your left. Go through a field gate and continue on a track which will bring you to Pityme, with The Pityme Inn just across the road.

You now have a choice. On my preferred route across fields, at the time of writing a footpath was to be diverted (for new development) so I can't give precise directions but I expect it will be well signed. If unadventurous, you could turn right along the main road towards Rock for 1km, then turn left at a crossroads into a housing development, and take the second on the right, LITTLE TRELYN. See below*.

Otherwise, continue ahead past the pub on PITYME FARM ROAD and follow it round to a T-junction. True, it's an industrial estate but more interesting than most!

*St Enodoc's Church – once so buried in the dunes that the clergyman was lowered through the roof for an annual service*

Turn right at the T-junction and just before Sharp's Brewery (which has a shop on-site) turn right, PUBLIC FOOTPATH, between industrial buildings. Walk diagonally across a yard to a stile.

Walk down the field with the hedge on your right. In the second field there's a stile in the middle of the bottom side, leading to a footbridge. There should now be signs for the diversion!

This will lead you to a private drive, where you turn right. At the lane turn left. At a T-junction, turn right. Ignore the footpath to your left and turn left into LITTLE TRELYN*.

At the far end continue along the footpath, keeping left when it forks, then turning left and immediately right at a street. You'll then be led into fields (until they're built over...) and the path is clear till you reach another housing development.

Continue down a street to a lane. Turn left and after 50 m right on PUBLIC FOOTPATH. At the beach you can cut across the little bay at low tide. Otherwise turn right as signed, walk up to the main road and turn left, which takes you past the Mariners Rock pub and on to the car park by the ferry access.

From the car park take COAST PATH POLZEATH, which leads into an area of dunes. Try to stick to the main waymarked path to minimise erosion. After passing a house, the path crosses a stream (after which a path on the right leads to the church of St Enodoc) then emerges onto the beach. Walk across the beach and up the steps to the Daymer Bay car park.

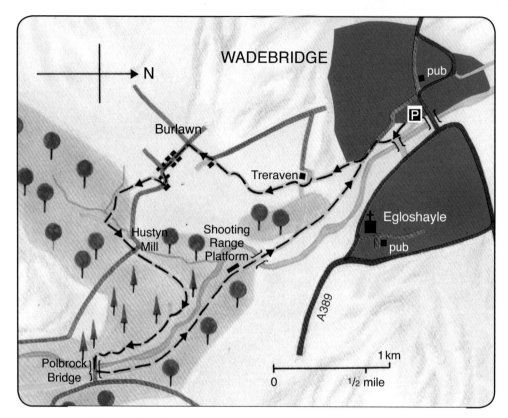

## Walk 3   Inland from Wadebridge

*Distance:  9.4km (5³/₄ miles)*

*Time:  2¹/₄ hours*

*Character: A deliberate contrast to the other walks in this book –
entirely inland, and through beautiful mixed woodland. Generally easy
walking, though one part of the walk (Treraven to Burlawn) can be
very muddy after a wet spell. It can be avoided by turning right at
Treraven, then left at a T-junction on a lane to Burlawn.*

Start from the Co-op car park in Wadebridge (SW991723) and head
inland along the riverside path. When you reach a street, turn left.
After 120m, when the Camel Trail proper starts, bear right up a track
(PUBLIC FOOTPATH TRERAVEN). At the end of the track, continue
ahead through a field with the hedge on your right, then go through
another gate into a track.

At a path junction (except in muddy conditions, see above) turn
left then bear right following the PUBLIC FOOTPATH signs. At the next
junction keep right, then follow a track (PUBLIC FOOTPATH) which

after 1 km arrives at a lane. Continue ahead to a crossroads, and turn left down into Burlawn.

Follow the main lane as it turns left then right, past an old pump. Opposite 'Hustyn Cottage' turn right (PUBLIC FOOTPATH), keep left through the entrance to 'Dumbles' then cross a stile and continue in the same direction across a field. At the very far side of the field a stile gives access to a woodland path which descends to the valley bottom.

Cross two footbridges, then turn left at the footpath junction. Keep left down beside Hustyn Mill to a lane. Turn right and almost immediately left into Bishops Wood.

Follow the broad and well-surfaced track, which after a time swings round to follow the Camel valley. After about 1 km, you will arrive at a bridge. Turn left across it, and descend steps to the Camel Trail. Beware cyclists! Turn left and follow the Trail back to Wadebridge.

You have a wide choice of pubs within Wadebridge, of which the historic Molesworth Arms Hotel in Molesworth Street (the main pedestrianised street) has the most interesting building.

If you would prefer a village pub with a collection of clocks, you could cross the footbridge and turn right along the road as far as Egloshayle church, then turn left behind the church and first right, for The Earl of St Vincent. That adds about 2 km to the walk.

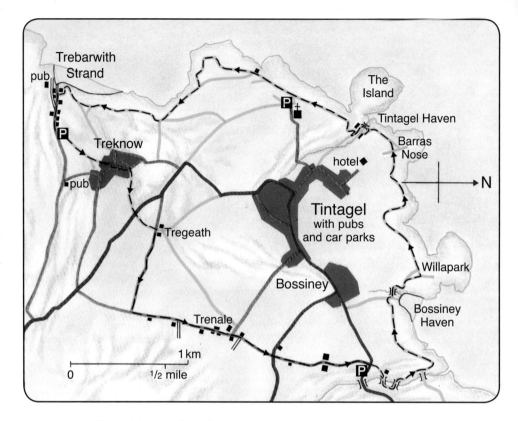

## Walk 4   Tintagel and the Port William Inn

*Distance: 12km (7¹/₂ miles)*
*Time: Allow 4 hours*
*Character: A walk of two contrasting halves: the cliff path includes
some of the most memorable scenery on Cornwall's dramatic coast, but
has several very steep ascents and descents. The inland section is
relatively easy, on footpaths and very quiet lanes.*

You could start from the large council car park at Trebarwith Strand
(SX053861) or from the small parking area by St Materiana's church
(though access can be a nightmare in summer), or from Tintagel village centre, but I have chosen to start from the small roadside parking
area at Rocky Valley (SX073890), because that gets the tough part of
the walk done first, with refreshment half way round.

From the parking area, walk up the road and bear right (PUBLIC
FOOTPATH) into the grounds of Trevillett Mill. Follow the signed path
into Rocky Valley, crossing the stream and recrossing it at ruined
Trewethett Mill, which apparently produced cloth and yarn from

12

around 1750 to 1861. Part of the site has been commandeered as a New Age shrine, on account of two carved labyrinths which some believe ancient, but which were more probably produced by bored mill apprentices.

After recrossing the stream, continue towards the sea, then bear left up a very steep stepped path. From the summit, follow the coast path. In several places the path divides: follow the route nearer the sea. On the way you will cross a steep-sided valley (more steps) and pass two headlands, Willapark and Barras Nose, both of which have paths leading out onto them.

At Barras Nose, continue ahead, GLEBE CLIFF. At Tintagel Haven, with its café, gift shop and toilets, cross the stream and turn inland, then turn right (COAST PATH). Zig-zag steeply up the valley side to the original castle entrance. Turn left, then right up a well-made stepped path, with views over Tintagel Island.

Approaching St Materiana's Church, bear right on the coast path, to pass the Youth Hostel. In the nineteenth century Glebe Cliff was extensively used as a slate quarry, and the Hostel was the manager's home and office. Take the seaward path and follow it round till you reach Trebarwith Strand. A steep descent leads to a lane. Cross over, passing a seasonal café, gift shops and public toilets, and bear right up

to the Port William Inn – which has the finest view from its terrace (see photo) of any pub I know.

From the pub, head inland down the access drive and join the lane. After 200 m, bear left through the large council car park and take the footpath at the far end, across the stream and up the opposite hillside to Treknow. At a path junction, continue ahead and keep left through a field. Go through a gate then walk past a row of cottages on your left.

At a T-junction, turn right past 'Briar Cottage', then very soon left uphill at another T-junction. Opposite Atlantic Close, turn right, PUBLIC FOOTPATH. Cross a complex double stile, then in the next field after 100 m turn left over a stile.

Bear right across the field to another stile near the top right corner. Cross the road with care and continue on PUBLIC FOOTPATH across two further fields to Tregeath Farm. You could continue on the footpath (see map) but I suggest turning right up the very quiet lane to a T-junction.

Turn left and follow the lane, with views over Tintagel, past Trebrea Lodge and Downrow to the hamlet of Trenale. Keep right at the triangular junction. On reaching a crossroads, go forward (HALGABRON) and follow the lane as it winds down through Halgabron to the Tintagel-Boscastle road. If you started at Rocky Valley, the parking area is on your right. Otherwise, cross the road into Trevillett Mill.

## Boscastle's pubs

In the early nineteenth century Boscastle was a busy little harbour town, effectively the port of Launceston and most of north Cornwall, exporting slate and manganese and importing just about everything that was needed. The population lived in the village up the hill, which was split between the parish of Minster, above the castle, and the parish of Forrabury from the castle down. The two parts of the harbour area were referred to as 'Bridge' and 'Quaytown', but not many people actually lived there.

There were many pubs, of different kinds. A local history suggests there were as many as twenty establishments selling alcohol in and around Boscastle, but from the evidence of the censuses I doubt that they were all operating at one and the same time.

In the 1841 census I found a total of 11, and by 1871 just 3 – the Napoleon, the Wellington and the Boscastle Inn (now 'Kiddlywink') at the top of Fore Street. In 1851 the upper town had two innkeepers and three 'victuallers' (providing food). Down at the Bridge, Ann Richard (aged 75) was a beer-seller at the 'Jessie Logan Inn'; Henry Mably ran the Ship Inn and John Bone ran an unnamed commercial hotel – probably the Joiner's Arms, which was extended and altered, and renamed the Wellington Hotel around 1853.

By 1856 William Bone, already a victualler in High Street in 1851, had named his pub the Napoleon. Presumably this was in response to the renaming of the Wellington, and a joke on his own name (Bonaparte was known as 'Boney'), but it is worth remembering that Wellington's reputation was as divisive as Margaret Thatcher's. As a soldier Wellington had won a victory at Waterloo, but as a politician he wanted to turn the clock back to the days of aristocratic rule. As prime minister he was so implacably opposed to electoral reform that we nearly had a revolution. Napoleon by contrast was (surprisingly) something of a hero in Britain after his defeat.

The Cobweb was built as a bonded warehouse and doubled as a wholesale outlet for alcohol and, from around 1920, as an off-licence known as the Launceston Cellar. It became a pub in 1947, at which time there were still massive cobwebs in the bar: they had been encouraged by the merchants as a way of keeping flies away from the barrels – but fear not, today Health & Safety prevails!

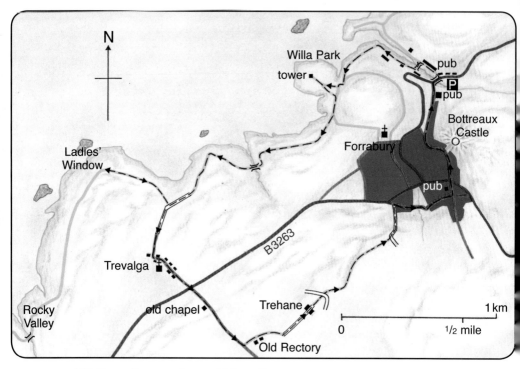

## Walk 5  Boscastle and Trevalga

*Distance: 8.2km (5 miles)*
*Time: 2¹/₄ hours*
*Character: Cliff path with moderate ascents, then quiet lanes and
inland paths for a rather rustic return. The walk visits both halves
of historic Boscastle, as well as the parish of Trevalga, sandwiched
between the honeypots of Boscastle and Tintagel, but in appearance at
least an unspoiled part of 'Old Cornwall'.*

From the car park in Boscastle walk down to the harbour. Cross the
river by the footbridge near the National Trust café and turn right
along the harbour. At the jetty, turn left uphill. At the entrance to Willa
Park, turn right up to the white Coastwatch station for the views.

Now return inland, noting the 'Forrabury stitches' (a medieval
strip field system) ahead of you. At a fork in the path bear right. Go
through a gate and turn right, rejoining the main coast path, and continue along the coast.

Nearing the hamlet of Trevalga a field gate leads into a waymarked
track towards the church, which you could take immediately, but I
recommend a diversion to the right, following the coast path for a

further 500 m to see an unusual rock formation, the Ladies' Window. It's just to your right at the top of a slope.

Now retrace your steps and turn right into the track and up to the churchtown of Trevalga. Turn left at the farm and follow the lane up to the main road. Cross into the lane ahead and climb past a disused chapel then steadily upward to 'The Old Rectory'.

Turn left, PUBLIC FOOTPATH. Pass around the buildings then turn right over a stile. At the far corner of a small field a gate gives access to a track towards Trehane Farm. Walk between the farmhouse to your left and a barn to your right.

Continue ahead, parallel to a hedge on your right, to a gateway. Then head diagonally across the next field to another gate, but don't go through it. Instead continue in the same direction with a ditch to your right. After 100 m turn right across the ditch by a footbridge.

A waymarked path now crosses two fields then descends to an access drive. Follow the drive downhill to a road junction, then turn right, PARADISE ROAD. Follow this across a valley to a crossroads, and turn left down HIGH STREET, passing the Napoleon Inn. At the crossroads continue down FORE STREET. (Just beyond the school, a brief diversion on the right will take you to the motte of Bottreaux Castle.)

At a fork, keep right downhill passing the Wellington Hotel, then turn right at the main road, back past The Cobweb to the car park.

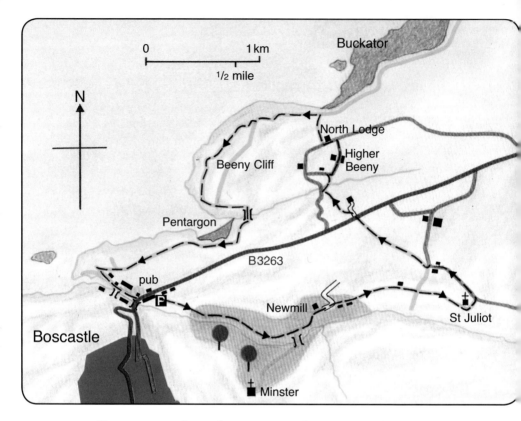

## Walk 6   Boscastle and Beeny – a Thomas Hardy walk

*Distance: 10 km (6 1/4 miles)*
*Time: 3 hours*
*Character: A woodland path beside a stream, a church restored by*
*Thomas Hardy (see page 20) then out to the coast path at its most*
*dramatic – Beeny Cliff and the waterfall at Pentargon. The last 2 km*
*of the walk are very strenuous.*

Leave the Boscastle car park by the footpath at the far end, NEWMILLS
ST JULIOTS, and walk beside the river for 1.2 km.

At the National Trust NEW MILLS sign, climb the steps, pass a cottage and continue up a track. Follow the waymarks and at Elm Cottage
bear left, signed ST JULIOT. The path soon begins to climb the valley
side and finally emerges from the woodland, and crosses two fields.

Cross a stone stile and continue with the hedge on your right till
you reach the church. Turn left into and through the churchyard out
to a lane. Turn left up the lane.

On reaching farm buildings and the entrance to the Old Rectory,

18

you have a choice. If it's muddy underfoot, or you don't fancy an imperfectly maintained footpath and stiles, then carry on along the lane. You could use lanes all the way to North Lodge – see sketch map – but take care on the B3263.

Alternatively, turn left towards the Old Rectory and immediately right over a wooden stile. Go through five fields to the B3263. Cross with care and continue towards Trebyla Farm. When the drive turns right, turn left over a stile then keep the hedge on your right for two fields, down to a lane.

Turn right and immediately right again, PUBLIC FOOTPATH. Climb steeply through one field, then straight up the next field towards a house. Turn right on the lane and follow it through Higher Beeny and past Manor Farm to a T-junction.

Turn left at the junction. After 100 m, beyond North Lodge, turn right TO THE COASTPATH. Entering a field, keep the hedge on your right, taking you out to the coast path at a particularly dramatic point. Turn left.

Entering Beeny Cliff, turn right PENTARGON – unless you suffer from vertigo or are at all unsteady on your feet, in which case continue on the optional path, because the coast path at this point makes some walkers nervous!

The paths converge at the foot of the slope. Then you climb again, and get your first view of Pentargon, with its waterfall. On the far side is a flight of steps leading up, and up. The word 'cliffhanger' may well owe its origin to this place: in Hardy's novel *A Pair of Blue Eyes*, which was first published as a serial in a magazine, one of the characters was left at the end of an instalment literally hanging by his fingernails from the cliff edge.

Once at the top, the coast path is relatively easy, till you reach the flagpole on Penally Point, from which you descend to Boscastle harbour. Walk up any of the harbourside routes, turn left on the main road, and you will pass The Cobweb as you enter the car park.

### Thomas Hardy in Cornwall

Thomas Hardy (1840-1928) came to Cornwall as a young architect to plan the restoration of St Juliot church. The Cornish coast worked its magic, and Hardy fell in love with Emma Gifford, the Rector's sister-in-law. The courtship was idyllic, the marriage rather less so; ultimately they separated. After Emma's death in 1912, Hardy revisited Cornwall and wrote some powerful poems about loss and regret, most notably 'Beeny Cliff'.

*Above right: The Bude Canal was unusual in that it was constructed to carry sand inland, rather than manufactured goods out to the coast. The lime-rich sand was valued as fertiliser.*

*The canal was opened in 1823. Tub boats were used, and they had wheels which allowed them to be hauled up or down six incline planes.*

*Below right: Marhamchurch, where the annual Revel takes place on the Monday after 12 August*

## Walk 7   Widemouth and Marhamchurch

*Distance:  10.3 km (6¹/₂ miles)*
*Time:  2³/₄ hours*
*Character: A very pleasant and relatively easy walk, with no steep ascents or descents. Mainly an inland walk, to the attractive village of Marhamchurch and the Bude Canal, including the remains of the incline plane. Some of the footpaths are unsigned. Some lane walking and one short stretch of the A39, so take care.*

Park at the free car park (SS199024) on the Bude side of Widemouth Bay, to the north of the Beach House Hotel. Walk out to Lower Longbeak point, then follow the coast path south to the beach.

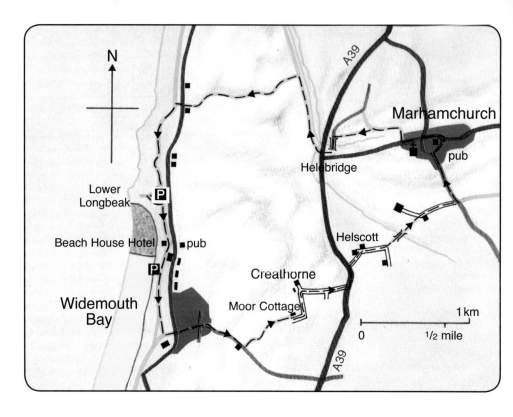

At the far end of the beach car park continue up the coast path for 100m, then bear left. About 200m before a holiday apartment complex, turn left on a well-beaten path up to the road. Cross into LEVERLAKE ROAD and follow it for 750m. Just beyond a thatched cottage, turn left into an enclosed track, which winds up to Moor Cottage.

From the house follow the concrete track, which turns sharp left then heads uphill towards Creathorne Farm. Turn right shortly before the farm, and ignore side turnings till you reach the main road. You may need to negotiate a vehicle barrier.

Turn left along the A39, taking great care. After 150m, turn right up a driveway signed to EAST HELSCOTT FARM etc. Bear right to pass East Helscott Cottage.

At a junction, turn left down to a gate and stile, then keep the hedge on your right. At the end of the field, turn right across two stiles to cross a footbridge, then head straight across the next field to a small bungalow. Turn right here up an access drive, which leads to a lane. Turn left along the lane into Marhamchurch.

Keep right within the village, to pass the Bullers Arms Hotel, and

turn left (west) past the crossroads, the church and the primary school. Then turn right, PLANEKEEPER'S PATH. This leads downhill parallel to the line of the incline plane. At a pumping station, turn left through a gate onto the plane itself. At the foot are the two boat bays: a noticeboard explains the technology used. Follow the towpath.

At Helebridge, turn left and immediately right (PUBLIC FOOTPATH) under the A39 and over footbridges. Turn right on the CANAL PATH. Pass a lock, then turn left, COAST PATH VIA COMMUNITY WOODLAND. This path winds up to the coast road. Cross over and walk out to the coast path, then turn left along it, back to the car park.

---

**The Bullers Arms**

The Bullers Arms, so-called since at least 1861, was probably named not after Sir Redvers Buller, the 'hero' (or incompetent general!) who relieved besieged Ladysmith in 1900, but after his great-uncle Sir Francis Buller, who acquired the Marhamchurch manor of Whaleborough in the 1790s, and became popularly known as 'Judge Thumb'. He apparently asserted that English law permitted a husband to thrash his wife with impunity provided the rod were no thicker than his thumb.

---

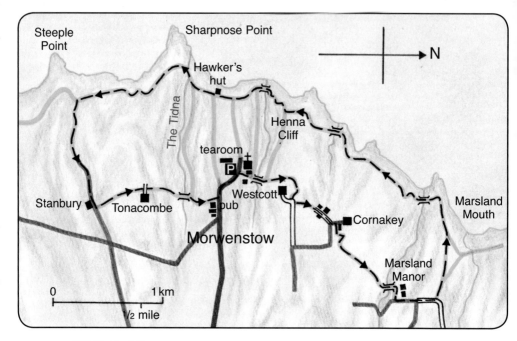

## Walk 8 Morwenstow

*Distance: 11.25km (7 miles) but can be shortened to under 8km*
*Time: 3 1/2 hours*
*Character: A strenuous but rewarding walk, with some very attractive inland scenery as well as magnificent cliffs. Several very steep ascents and descents.*

Start from the car park between Morwenstow church and the Rectory Tearoom. Go through the lych gate, immediately turn right down a path with a rail and follow waymarks through the Old Vicarage grounds.

Ignore a path to the left and cross a footbridge. Emerging from the wooded valley, continue ahead and in the second field follow ALTERNATIVE PATH AVOIDING FARM YARD, one of several such on this walk. Cross a stile at the top of the field and turn right. Jink right and left, which will bring you to the farm access drive.

To its left are two gates: go through the right hand gate and keep the hedge on your left. Pass to the right of a house. At a lane junction, turn left and after 50m turn right as signed, then left through a gate and right along a track. After a field gate, the path cuts diagonally across fields heading straight for Marsland Manor.

Cross a wooded valley, then turn right across a paddock as signed. Turn right as signed into the lower field, then left along its upper edge

24

and out to a lane. Turn left along the lane to pass Marsland Manor. At the top of a slope, continue ahead, UNSUITABLE FOR MOTORS. When you reach the notice board for the Marsland Valley Nature Reserve, turn left on a waymarked path, then bear left at a fork.

This leads out to join the coast path (unsigned but obvious) which you now follow to and past Morwenstow – though as you begin the descent from Henna Cliff, the first of several potential short-cuts offers itself to your left (see map). Hawker's hut, where the famous vicar contemplated the ocean, is on your right at the top of Vicarage Cliff, after which the coast path descends steeply to the Tidna valley. An inland path leads up the valley and is your last chance of a short cut!

Otherwise, continue on the coast path up to Sharpnose Point (we definitely don't recommend walking out on it!) then continue with the GCHQ radio station ahead of you to an area of cliff falls, where the coast path veers right. Instead, turn inland through a gate (waymarked). The path becomes a track then a lane and leads to Stanbury farm.

Opposite the farm turn left (PUBLIC FOOTPATH) and cross the field to the middle of the far side (gate and stile) then over the next field heading just to the left of the farm complex.

Cross a farm track and follow the waymarked path in more or less a straight line, through innumerable pedestrian gates and down into a valley. Bear right at the foot, CROSSTOWN, and climb steps. Climb a small field to another gate, then pass through the Bush Inn's garden and up to the lane. Turn left along the lane, back to the church.

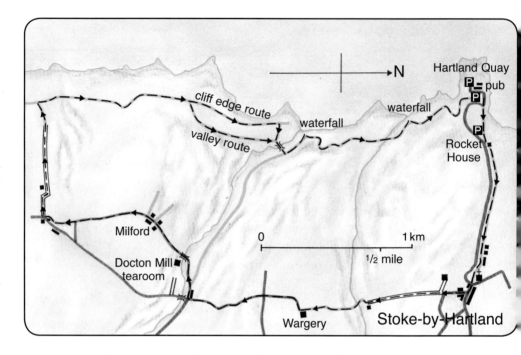

## Walk 9  Hartland Quay and Docton Mill

*Distance:  9km (5½ miles)*
*Time:  2¼ hours*
*Character: Starting with pleasant footpaths and very quiet lanes, and finishing with coastal scenery which becomes ever more dramatic as you approach Hartland Quay, with its hotel/pub. The walk also passes the Docton Mill tearoom, which does lunches as well as teas.*

Park at Hartland Quay (toll road in lieu of parking charge) and walk back up the cliff by the stepped path, to the toll booth and 'Rocket House'. Now head back towards Stoke. There's no need to walk on the lane, which gets busy in season: a footpath runs along the edge of the field on the left, parallel to the lane, then continues across the fronts of houses as far as the church.

Cross into the churchyard, bear right around the church and leave by a lych gate. Walk ahead along the lane for 30m, then turn right at 'Rose Cottage'. This unsigned lane becomes a track labelled UNSUITABLE FOR MOTORS, and after a time the tarmac does indeed disintegrate.

At Wargery farm, keep right and continue to a crossroads. Take

26

the lane ahead, ELMSCOTT WELCOMBE. At the foot of the valley turn right at the crossroads, MILFORD. Cross the stream beside Docton Mill (refreshments) and climb to Milford.

Ignore the footpaths off to the right and continue along the lane for a further 700 m. When the lane turns left, continue ahead, PUBLIC FOOTPATH. At the end of the field cross a stile, pass behind the house and descend to a lane. Turn right along a concrete drive, PUBLIC FOOTPATH.

The drive zigzags, then becomes a track heading west, ending one field short of the coast. Head as signed to the far left corner of the field and turn right, COAST PATH SPEKES MILL. Follow the path till it divides.

The inland COAST PATH VALLEY ROUTE is easier walking and considerably safer. The CLIFF TOP FOOTPATH, initially a track across grassland, turns into a cliff edge path unsuitable for vertigo sufferers, with quite a difficult descent – but the views are fantastic! If you do take the cliff path, turn right, down across the valley, when the opportunity presents, rejoining the main path, crossing the stream by a footbridge and turning left, HARTLAND QUAY.

After 150 m, the Spekes Mill waterfall is on your left, one of the most spectacular on the whole South West Coast Path. The path

now climbs steeply before descending again into a dry valley behind St Catherine's Tor (also called St Catherine's Point), with another waterfall at the far end, then up another slope back to the car parks at Hartland Quay.

## Walk 10   Hartland Point and Quay

*Distance: 10 km (6¹/4 miles)*
*Time: 3 hours*
*Character: Ancient farm tracks lead parallel to the coast as far as Stoke, where St Nectan's church is a land and sea mark, then dramatic rocky formations along the coast path make this a very memorable walk – though quite a challenging one, with numerous ascents and descents, several of them steep enough for steps.*

Start from the car park at Hartland Point (SS 235275). Return up the access lane. When the lane turns left, continue ahead PUBLIC BRIDLEWAY BLEGBERRY. The track bears right through Blagdon Farm, then descends into a valley. At a path junction, turn left, BLEGBERRY.

> **Hartland Quay** dates from the late 16th century. It was the trading port for the area, and was leased to 'the Merchant'. By the 1890s trade was declining, but the beauty of the setting was attracting tourists. An addendum slip in my 1894 edition of *The Thorough Guide* (printed in 1892) says that 'the Hartland Quay Hotel (about 10 bedrooms and some stabling) has been opened by T Oatway, for many years the driver of the mail-brake between Bideford, Clovelly and Hartland.'

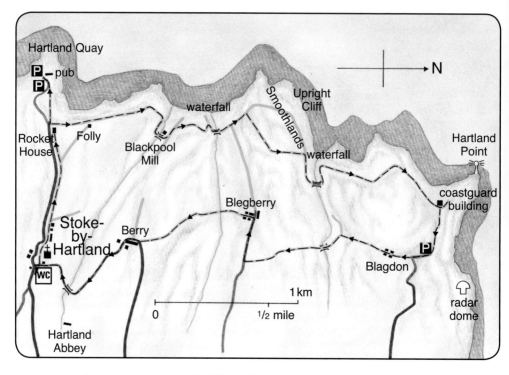

Cross a stream and follow the track up as far as a lane. Turn right along it to Blegberry Farm, then turn left in front of the barns (UNSUITABLE FOR MOTOR VEHICLES). The lane soon becomes a winding muddy track, crossing another valley and rising to another lane.

This time continue ahead, again signed UNSUITABLE FOR MOTOR VEHICLES. The lane winds left then right through Berry then descends to pass Hartland Abbey on your left, before winding up the hill to Stoke-by-Hartland.

Turn right into the churchyard (PUBLIC FOOTPATH) past the church. From the far side of the churchyard a footpath leads across the front of a terrace of cottages, then continues parallel to the lane. Pass more houses then keep the hedge on your left through fields.

Continue as far as a small building, the Rocket House (where life-saving equipment was formerly housed). Turn left onto the lane, and either follow the driveway past the toll booth and gently downward, or plunge ahead down the COAST PATH. Either way brings you to the quay car parks.

After visiting the Quay – which has a seasonal shop and a shipwreck museum as well as the pub, the remains of the quay itself and some

exceptional geology – climb back up the hill and turn left immediately before the Rocket House (COAST PATH). Pass the Folly (which may have started life as a medieval building).

On its way to Hartland Point, the coast path crosses several steep-sided valleys. Descending towards the first valley, the path cuts back on itself; turn left at a signed junction to pass inland of Blackpool Mill. Then turn left, and after 50 m bear right up a steep slope.

At the next valley, a PUBLIC FOOTPATH to the left leads down to Blegberry Beach, but a diversion of just a few metres along it gives a good view of a waterfall.

At the top of the next climb, ignore a footpath off towards Blegberry. Then at the next junction, where the coast path continues ahead, turn right PUBLIC FOOTPATH. This route follows the rim of the valley, giving a wonderful view (and it just happens to be easier walking!) before it rejoins the coast path.

Turn right at the junction, descend across yet another valley, again with a waterfall, and continue along the coast path until you reach a coastguard building surmounted with a radio mast.

Just behind this building a short diversion leads to a fantastic view of Hartland Point and its lighthouse, with Lundy beyond. We recommend you do not venture out onto the Point itself. A further 400 m along the coast path brings you back to the car park.

## Suggestions for there-and-back walks

### 11 Port Quin and Port Isaac
Park at Port Quin (SW 972805) and walk the coast path to Port Isaac, with a choice of pubs. This is a seriously demanding section of coast path, and the walk is 5 km each way. (An 8 km circular version can be found in *Shortish Walks in north Cornwall*.)

### 12 Port Isaac and beyond Port Gaverne
Start from the main car park at Port Isaac and walk east along the coast, then return to the delightful bar of the Port Gaverne Inn.

### 13 Crackington Haven
Park at Crackington Haven (SX 143968), where there is a pub as well as a café, and walk the coast path west to Cambeak and then south to High Cliff. (A 7.3 km circular version of this walk can be found in *Shortish Walks in north Cornwall*.)

## Some other Bossiney walks books you might find useful

*North Devon pub walks* (8-18 km)

*Shortish Walks in north Cornwall* (5-8 km)
*Shortish Walks in north Devon* (5-9 km)

*Walks on High Dartmoor* (7-20 km)

For a full list of our walks books please see our website,
www.bossineybooks.com